TRANSWOMEN DESTROYING THE COMPETITION

An Essay showing how Transwomen have an Unfair Advantage in Women's Only Sports

Liam Schwartz

CONTENTS

TRANSWOMEN DESTROYING THE COMPETITION

THE END OF WOMEN'S SPORTS

Do you think it's fair that transwomen get to destroy women's sports? So much for Progressives being compassionate! transwomen are claiming to be women to enjoy the benefits that come with being a woman. By claiming to be women they can get the best of both worlds: especially in sorts where they can easily beat cis women.

Transgender people are people who identify as a gender other than the one typically associated with their biological sex. Societal pressure exists for transgendered people to live as members of their identified sex in terms of clothing, name, and pronouns. This pressure comes both from society at large and from transgendered people themselves.

I would like to discuss the ways in which transwomen have an advantage, with the goal of increasing awareness that their advantage must be considered when determining whether or not to include trans athletes competing against cis-athletes in the same category. I want to preface this by saying that my motivation is not rooted in a desire for fairness, but rather a desire for functional fairness.

In the recent past, the IAAF has updated its regulations to cover trans athletes. This was in response to rising complaints about transgender unfairness so that not only were they required to have their testosterone levels below a certain threshold but also required to remain at said level for at least 6 months.

In the past, this advantage was easy to ignore and downplay because the numbers of trans people were small, or at least looked small. Now that more and more people are coming out and transitioning, we can no longer deny these advantages of transwomen:

Athletes at the Idaho State University have joined lawsuits against transwomen's participation in women's sports. They're represented by the conservative legal advocacy organization Alliance Defending Freedom. They've said their position is not based on hate or anti-trans sentiment but about fairness and opportunity in their sport. Some of them claim to have lost out on chances because of losing out on races they consider unfair. They are seeking to overturn a policy that would let transwomen compete in women's sports. These athletes aren't alone in their backlash against the International Olympics Committee's decision to open up women's events to the transgendered."

In this book I am going to break down the various advantages that transwomen have over biological women, and how their participation in the same events as cis women may be a disadvantage to the cis women. I'll take several other related topics of current debate and examine their positions in relation to trans-genderism and some other topics of interest to the overall discussion.

Advantages I am going to point out are not exactly exclusive to trans-women. If they were solely a biological phenomenon, it would be easier to prove it without looking at observational data or surveys. These advantages are involved in the dynamic between transwomen and cis women because they have less opportunity and resources available to them than cis women do. This is an undeniable fact that cannot be ignored or overlooked even if we all agree that transwomen are biologically different from cis women.

INTRODUCTION

As the transgender community becomes more visible, more people are questioning their obvious advantage over biological women. For example, their involvement in competitive sport has come under greater scrutiny. Critics assert that transwomen have an unfair advantage over biological women because they have had male hormones coursing through their body before puberty. They contend that the increased level of testosterone creates a significant and unfair advantage in both muscle mass and aerobic capacity.

Recently, there has been some fuss about transgender athletes and how they have an unfair advantage over biological females in sports competitions. The IAAF Eligibility Regulations for the Female Classification (Athletes with Differences of Sex Development) issued directions on participation of transwomen in International sports. These Regulations set the criteria for participation of athletes who have a Difference of Sexual Development (DSD). DSD refers to levels of testosterone. To be considered eligible to compete in for events in 400m to one mile, the athletes have to meet the following criteria:

a. they must be recognized legally as female or intersex

b. they must maintain a blood testosterone level of five nmol/L or below for a at least 6 months

c. thereafter, they must maintain this level continuously for as long as they want to be eligible.

This means that any transwomen who wish to compete in these international games have to take active steps to reduce their testosterone by use of hormone replacement therapy.

Athletes like Caster Semenya who have Hyperandrogenism (excessive production of Testosterone) have not been allowed to race in the female categories. The European Association for Olympic Sports also has rules in place barring biological women with hyperandrogenism from competing against women.

EXAMINING THE BIOLOGICAL ADVANTAGES MALES HAVE OVER FEMALES

There are three factors contributing to a major physical advantage: biological differences, physical advantages and hormone levels. with regard to biological differences, there are three points which will be looked at in detail below: height, testosterone levels and muscle mass. Height is one of the most obvious differences between transwomen and biological women. Biological females don't grow any taller than 5 feet 9 inches, whereas transwomen can reach 6 feet in height or even higher. There are many other traits which indicate that transwomen have an advantage over biological females, but height is obviously the most obvious and easy to demonstrate. The primary hormone responsible for tallness is testosterone. It is well known that testosterone has extensive effects on human growth and development. So where does this go wrong when it comes to transwomen? Biological females not only have testosterone coursing through their veins, but also estrogen coursing through theirs, which equates to a huge peak level of estrogen in the blood. It is likely that this high level of estrogen confuses the growth process so that they develop at least 1 or 2 inches taller than ordinary biological women.

There are other differences between transwomen and biological females which will be considered in more detail later: muscle mass and aerobic capacity. Due to their high testosterone levels, transgender women have a significant increase in lean body mass. In contrast, biological females at similar ages have a much lower percentage of lean body mass, meaning that their muscle mass is much less than that of transwomen. Another difference between transwomen and biological females is the ability to sustain endurance. Unfortunately, too many studies rely upon small sample sizes with insufficient data for statistical analysis. The results from those that do are quite clear though. Biological females have a significantly lower maximum oxygen uptake (VO2 max) than transwomen. This is due to lower levels of hemoglobin, red blood cells and plasma volume, which all contribute to lower aerobic capacity.

Aside from the biological differences, transwomen have some physical advantage over biological women. These advantages manifest in strength, endurance and size. It has been suggested that transwomen possess greater muscle mass and strength partly due to their higher testosterone levels. The increase in muscle mass is likely due to the fact that transwomen have more testosterone coursing through their veins. Furthermore, as mentioned above, their height can be attributed to testosterone because estrogen will obstruct the natural process. There is also evidence that testosterone plays a fundamental role in endurance as well. Endurance can be described as the ability to sustain exercise for a long period of time. With their higher levels of testosterone, transwomen are more likely to possess greater endurance than biological females. As is consistent with males who have lower hemoglobin levels, transwomen will have lower heart rates and less efficient utilization of oxygen, giving them a further endurance advantage. Research by Subashini et al., 2007 has shown that blood pressure and cardiac output are lower in transwomen than biological females when performing physical exercise at 70% VO2 max. The study also showed that transwomen's hearts did not contract at the same rate as biological females during a stress test.

Finally, size is a feature which transwomen possess over biological females. In general, transwomen are more muscular and larger than biological females in most adult stages. It seems that the addition of testosterone to a person's body during puberty, as is the case with transwomen, causes them to have an advantage over biological females. This effect is more prominent in the muscles than in other areas, so size is an advantageous trait which transwomen possess. However, it should be noted that transgender men are not biologically male.

ANDROGEN IS LINKED TO INCREASED LEVELS OF CONFIDENCE AND DOMINANCE

Other than the advantages listed above, psychological differences between the genders also exist. This is what leads to the claim that transgender women are biologically better put together than biological women. These psychological differences include: gender role socialization (the way that males and females conform their behavior to perceived gender roles), skeletal morphology (differences in bone structure), hormonal profile (levels of testosterone and estrogen) and endocrine system development (hormones such as estrogen can masculinize the brain). Gender role socialization has been shown to play a major role in how an individual's body develops.

Basically, the differences between men and women are down to the levels of testosterone produced by both. When testosterone levels are high in women it will result in increased muscle mass, more body hair, deeper voices etc. women with higher levels of testosterone will appear more masculine but they will still be female. In contrast when male testosterone levels are low they become more feminine (less body hair etc) and develop a higher pitched voice. Men with lower levels of testosterone will appear more feminine and be considered less male.

Similarly, men also have a higher level of testosterone whereas females have relatively low levels, i.e., the 'ballistic' effect on the musculature of men is much greater than that of women. Transwomen will therefore have a higher level of testosterone than the average biological woman, albeit not as high as biological males, so they will have a degree of musculature and bone structure which is more developed than that of biological females.

The fact that transwomen possess relatively high levels of testosterone in comparison to biological females will not, however, explain all the differences between men and women. There are numerous other physical differences which are clearly evident in transgender women but not in biological females. These include: shorter hip bones, larger breasts, smaller feet, different anatomical proportions of the body (such as longer torsos), increased muscularity (especially in the upper body), shorter stature and a narrower pelvis. If we compare these differences with those observed in males this becomes even more obvious.

This book will explore the science of gender, examine how transwomen construct their identities, explore how they fare under current anti-doping policy, and look at the impacts on women's sport if transgender competitors are allowed to compete without restrictions in non-transgender competitions.

CHAPTER 1: ANDROGEN

What is Androgen?

Androgens are a group of hormones that play a role in male traits and reproductive activity. Present in both males and females, the principal androgens are testosterone and androstenedione. Testosterone, arguably the most important of the androgens, is present in both males and females but in much higher levels in males. It is generally considered the most important androgen secreted by the testes; it plays a major role in the sexual differentiation of individuals, influencing reproductive function, mood, muscle mass, aggression and libido. Testosterone has numerous effects on human physiology including growth, bone-building, fat distribution and body hair. Testosterone levels are dependent on age as well as other factors such as diet. They decline with age in women but remain a factor in all men over 50 years old because of its effect on bone-building.

Testosterone and other androgens are secreted by the testes, ovaries, adrenal cortex, the gonads of external sex organs (the two testes in males and the ovaries in females), the adrenal cortex of gonads (the male testes) and by cells of the prostate gland.

Secondary male sex hormones include Androstenedione and Dihydrotestosterone (DHT). Androstenedione (aka androstenedione) is an adrenal precursor of testosterone in males. Dihydrotestosterone (aka dihydrotestosterone), is a metabolite of testosterone that can convert to estrogen in the body and which often causes breast development in biological males.

In biological males, testosterone levels will increase during puberty, whereupon it will remain high for the rest of their life. It should be noted that during puberty boys also develop other sex hormones such as estrogen and progesterone, however this does not typically occur during adulthood unless there is some abnormality or dysfunction with their gonads.

in women testosterone levels are usually much lower than that of men. In children, both boys and girls have about the same level of testosterone. As they enter puberty, girls begin to produce less testosterone. Females who aren't producing enough testosterone are "more susceptible to mood swings and tenderness as well as have a higher risk for developing osteoporosis," says Sue Henken, PhD, a professor of behavioral science at Case Western Reserve University in Cleveland.

In transwomen they will have levels of testosterone similar to biological men but not quite as high thus they will have a body that is more muscular yet less bulky than biological men. They will have a smaller amount of body hair and lower levels of testosterone. This will help them to have a lighter voice, more feminine bone structure, wider hips and more breast tissue. In some cases, they may even have natural breasts.

HOW DOES ANDROGEN WORK IN THE BODY?

Androgen binds to androgen receptors in target tissues such as bone, muscle, liver, brain, heart and kidney. It can either increase or reduce transcription of specific genes depending on the receptor density. This is how it influences height and bone-mass as well as muscle mass. If there are many receptors in a particular tissue then it is more sensitive to androgens than other parts of the body.

If there are more androgen receptors than target cells they will bind with testosterone or dihydrotestosterone (DHT) more readily. This results in the formation of a complex which will then enter the nucleus and bind to DNA at certain locations known as hormone response elements (HREs).

HOW DO TRANSWOMEN HAVE AN ADVANTAGE OVER WOMEN DUE TO ANDROGEN?

From the above text it is clear that androgen has a major role in humans. These hormones play an important part in the physical maturation of males and females. For example, they play a role in male pattern baldness, muscle development and bone mass as well as sex drive among other things.

In male bodies testosterone is important during puberty when it contributes to sex drive and muscle growth. In transgender women this hormone will produce many of the same effects as in biological males and will contribute to their masculinizing features such as muscle mass and height. They will have a much higher testosterone level than women but not as high as men. This will help them to exhibit masculine features even if they are biologically female like wider hips and more breast tissue.

In sports, this difference in testosterone between transwomen and biological women will appear as:

They will have a lower fat percentage due to having higher levels of testosterone. As we learned before, testosterone increases lean body mass while reducing fat mass. This is a result of the testosterone binding to androgen receptors in target tissue causing them to become more active and increase gene expression. The result is increased lean body mass that will translate to more endurance, speed and agility. Biological women with a higher body fat percentage have greater resistance to athletic motion. This forces the athlete to increase the muscle force of construction per workload. The result is a limit on their endurance, balance, coordination and movement capacity.

Transwomen will have a higher VO2 max than biological women. VO2 max is the maximum amount of oxygen that is consumed by the body during physical exercise. the greater your VO2 max is, the more oxygen you can consume to produce energy during exercise. The higher your VO2 max the better your endurance is. A higher level will allow them to have a greater endurance capacity and also as a result of this, another advantage over biological women is there will be less fatigue in those muscles which will lead to greater speed and agility. This comes from the improved metabolism of these athletes. They will also have a lower rate of lactate accumulation in muscle tissue resulting in higher power output which again is due to higher levels of testosterone allowing better muscle recovery and increased speed.

Testosterone makes men more aggressive through its effect on androgen receptors in the brain. A study done by T.S Bruce et al in 1988 showed that men had a higher level of aggression than women. Testosterone increased this difference. Men with more testosterone were also shown to be more willing to fight. aggression in sports is a very important aspect of competition. A transwoman will have the advantage in this area because of their higher level of testosterone.

Trans athletes will have a greater muscle mass and strength than their biological female counterparts. Testosterone's close relationship with protein synthesis plays a role in muscle growth. As androgen is produced by the testes and is responsible for the development and function of muscles, it would make sense that increased testosterone would result in greater muscle growth than women would experience without these hormones. In male bodies, testosterone is responsible for the creation and medical maintenance of muscle mass. As mentioned before, as testosterone increases, so does muscle mass. So even if a transwoman has some of the advantages listed above, she still has the advantage over biological females because of her higher level of testosterone.

This HRE is very important for regulating cell growth and division. Testosterone can also affect the formation of DNA in certain areas of the body, especially in the brain and spinal cord (HREs that are important in regulating cell growth). This will lead to more aggressive behavior traits as well as physical strength due to more muscle mass.

Do transwomen have an unfair advantage due to androgen?

A study on transgender athletes has found transwomen retain a 12% advantage in running tests even after taking hormones for two years to suppress their testosterone. The results, researchers suggest, indicate the current International Olympic Committee guidelines may give transwomen an "unfair competitive advantage" over cis women. The researchers measured anaerobic capacity, speed, and time taken to cover a four kilometer course on a downhill treadmill. Before their transition, the transwomen tested faster than females in the control group by 12%

However, this advantage lessens the longer that an athlete is on HRT. This is because suppression of testosterone results in a decrease in muscle mass and muscle strength. Again, this will result in a lesser advantage.

CHAPTER 2: ADVANTAGE IN SPORTS

THE TESTOSTERONE ADVANTAGE NEVER DISAPPEARS

transwomen are biologically female but have an advantage in many sports. This advantage is not due to being born in the wrong body or having an unfair advantage over biological females but rather from having a naturally high testosterone level. A study on transgender athletes has found transwomen retain a 12% advantage in running tests even after taking hormones for two years to suppress their testosterone. The results, researchers suggest, indicate the current International Olympic Committee guidelines may give transwomen an "unfair competitive advantage" over ciswomen. The researchers measured anaerobic capacity, speed, and time taken to cover a four-kilometer course on a downhill treadmill. Before their transition, the transwomen tested faster than females in the control group by 12%

But after two years their advantage was only 3%. These results indicate that testosterone never disappears completely, causing transwomen to retain a competitive advantage against their biological female counterparts.

Testosterone does not just increase physical strength; it also improves speed and endurance. This results in an advantage in sports where these attributes are important. An advantage can be seen in sports like track and field events like sprinting or the 400m clearing. It is well known that sprinters are born with their incredible speed so this shows that this is not an unfair advantage since they were born with it.

A study was done to help understand whether the performance of transwomen athletes differed from that of biological males and females. The results showed a clear difference in performance between the different sexes during specific tasks, which led researchers to believe that hormones may play a role in these differences. Specifically, there was an improvement observed among transwomen during short treadmill running tests (<4 minutes) than among both males and females. However, when comparing the four-kilometer test, there was no difference between the performance of transwomen and biological females or males. The study concluded that while hormones may contribute to performance differences between transwomen and their biological sex counterparts, certain tasks which are critical for sports are affected by testosterone.

Trans athletes have advantages in sports where muscle is important. For example in sports like track and field events (sprinting and high jumping) where speed and muscle mass are necessary. Also, a huge advantage would be in basketball where physical strength and stamina is important.

Transwomen retain athletic edge after a year of hormone replacement therapy

The study by the University of Stirling, published in the American Journal of Sports Medicine, looked at transwomen athletes who had a year since starting hormone replacement therapy (HRT) to show whether or not their strength and lactate threshold had improved. The study measured their performance during four kilometers on a downhill treadmill and compared their results with that of biological female athletes.

The results are interesting as they show that even after only 2 years of hormone therapy transwomen have reduced their advantage over biological women from 12% to 6%. This reduction is due to transwomen reducing their muscle mass while increasing fat mass after two years on hormone therapy. Reducing muscle mass reduces speed as it reduces the force generated by skeletal muscles which is necessary for moving limbs as fast as possible in sports such as running.

The transgender women were found to have less muscle mass than biological females but had a higher aerobic capacity. This test is known as anaerobic threshold. The study concluded that despite having less muscle mass these transwomen retained an athletic edge over biological females due to an increased aerobic capacity. The study also found that after one year of HRT, the average difference in performance between trans athletes and biological females got smaller. This can be confirmed by a study conducted by the University of California, San Francisco which states that Transwomen are faster after a year of hormone treatment. Hormones have an effect on the muscle mass of transwomen and how it is distributed. These changes affect their athletic performance.

Athletic performance is affected by testosterone, but hormone levels also affect muscle mass and bone density. After two years of taking hormones for transgender woman, muscle mass begins to decrease. After four years of taking hormones, transwomen have lost their muscle mass and gained fat. This trend has been seen in athletes such as Becks Eckert who has been a transgender woman for eleven years and used testosterone for six of those eleven years to change her body shape from male to female. She has successfully competed in several competitive sports meet despite the loss of muscle mass and fat accumulation which is typical after two years of hormone therapy indicating that there are significant differences between transgender women with and without testosterone replacement therapy.

CHAPTER 3: STRENGTH

Testosterone is important for muscle growth, so a transwomen will have a lower fat percentage and more lean body mass due to her higher level of testosterone. The effects of testosterone on muscle increase as testosterone receptors in the muscles become more sensitive. Testosterone increases lean body mass and reduces fat mass. This leads to reduced estrogen levels resulting in less fat, greater muscle mass and increased strength for transwomen.

MUSCLE SIZE VARIES BY GENDER

Testosterone is a steroid hormone, which is created in the testes of males and ovaries of females. The concentration of testosterone in males is 10-fold greater than that found in females. This sex difference can be attributed to the fact that males produce approximately 4–6 times higher concentrations of androgens than females. An interesting aspect of testosterone can be seen from the study by Mueller et al, (1998) which found that male sex hormones are essential for skeletal muscle force generation during explosive contractions at high loads. Even though testosterone plays an important role in muscle growth, most studies have focused on its action as an androgen to maintain secondary male sexual characteristics or to support bone health. This knowledge of testosterone has been applied in practices such as hormone replacement therapy (HRT), which is aimed at reducing age-related bone loss and maintaining skeletal muscle function in older adults.

Testosterone levels also affect muscle performance, as seen in women with low levels of testosterone who have been linked to poor athletic performance. Wilson et al (1997) suggests there is a "ceiling" effect beyond which increasing androgen administration will not increase physical performance. It is important to take into account that testosterone/androgens are most effective when administered at an early stage of development. In order to understand how hormones affect the muscular system, we must consider the fact that there are no clear cut-off points between male and female skeletal muscles. This is mainly due to the fact that skeletal muscle is highly susceptible to androgenic modulation and has a certain degree of plasticity. For example, the male skeletal muscle contains more androgen receptor sites than the female skeletal muscle, while at the same time male skeletal muscle is also less sensitive to androgens than female muscles. It has been suggested that testosterone can have an effect on several features of skeletal muscles such as fiber-type composition, myosin isozyme composition, myosin heavy chain gene expression, oxidative enzyme activity, capillary supply density and mitochondrial size. This shows us that testosterone plays a major role in regulating muscular development from both sexes.

It is important to consider factors that affect muscularity when speaking about athletic performance. Hormone levels are one of the most important factors in athletic performance as testosterone plays a key role in muscular development and strength. It is important to understand that testosterone is detected in higher concentrations in males, but this does not mean that females cannot have high levels of testosterone.

Although estrogen and progesterone are associated with increased fat accumulation, they still increase muscle growth through their effects on androgen receptors. Estrogen increases muscle mass by enhancing sensitivity of the cells to testosterone. It does this by increasing the concentration of androgen receptors within the muscle tissue which results in greater uptake of free-testosterone within their cells leading to greater muscle mass for transwomen than biological women even when they have similar testosterone levels. Estrogen is also responsible for female body shape and increased fat deposition. Estrogen has an effect on muscularity, although it is controversial as to whether this is through a direct effect or indirectly through the effect on fat deposition and muscle size.

This will be a very important factor when comparing transwomen and biological women in sports. Transwomen will have an advantage over biological women because even if they do not have as much muscle mass as ciswomen, they still have greater bone density due to their higher levels of testosterone, resulting in improved strength and bone health for transwomen. This shows that there are many factors to consider when determining whether an athlete is at a disadvantage or advantage. When speaking about testosterone in athletic performance, it is important to consider the multiple factors that promote greater muscle growth.

This HRE is important because skeletal muscles make up a large part of the body mass and are responsible for locomotion, posture and supporting the skeleton. So, there is a clear advantage in sports like running or power lifting since transwomen have a larger skeletal muscle mass than biological women. Endocrine disruptors like estrogen have been linked with an increase in fat accumulation. This can be beneficial for women because it can increase their fat-free mass, while at the same time reducing their fat mass. Estrogen promotes skeletal muscle mass and works synergistically with testosterone. For transwomen, the average difference in performance between trans athletes and biological females got smaller when measured across disciplines in track and field, swimming, rowing, football and basketball after hormone therapy had been administered for 1 year.

Another factor to consider is the distribution of the muscle mass. Transwomen on hormone therapy have more muscle mass in the lower body and less in the upper body compared to biological women. This trend can be seen in sports like basketball, football, swimming, rowing and weightlifting where power production or muscle strength is important for success. Transwomen have a greater percentage of their skeletal muscles located in their lower body compared to biological women. Scientists suggest that this may be because transwomen retain an advantage when lifting weights where total weight is lifted and not just the force generated by muscles. This shows that there are many factors to consider when determining whether an athlete is at a disadvantage or advantage when they are using hormones for athletic performance improvement.

Transwomen are considered to have an advantage over biological women in several sports because they have a greater muscle mass in their lower body and less in the upper body compared to biological women. This trend can be seen in sports like basketball, football, swimming, rowing and weightlifting where power production or muscle strength is important for success. Transwomen have a greater percentage of their skeletal muscles located in their lower body compared to biological women.

Testosterone also has an effect on bone density which is another factor affecting athletic performance. Testosterone promotes bone mineralization by stimulating the osteoblastic cells that form bone and it also modulates osteoclastic activity (bone resorption). This is an important aspect to consider when assessing the athletic performance of transwomen as a lower bone density would decrease their strength and speed when performing certain activities. This HRE will also affect physical performance. For example, the masculine bone structure is more resistant to fracture than that of a biological woman. Transwomen have a higher bone density than biological women and this can be seen in the study by Kestens et al. (2010) in which transwomen had a lower risk of hip and knee fractures when compared to biological women due to their greater bone density.

This is of great relevance when assessing the athletic performance of transwomen because it affects how their muscles contract, how fast they move and how much momentum their body has. It is especially important for transwomen who participate in sports that require a high level of physical performance like running or power lifting.

Another factor that should be considered when evaluating transwomen as athletes is the reduction in muscle mass after two years of hormone therapy. Muscle plays an important role in athletic performance since it plays a role in determining speed and strength which are crucial for successful performance in many sports. Researchers found that although hormones may affect athletic performance, there are certain tasks which are affected differently by testosterone than others. For example, in high intensity sprinting, male athletes have more power than female athletes. In contrast, both male and female sprinters have the same maximum speed. Researchers found that testosterone is not as important for explosive contractions as it is for strength. This study shows that performance is affected differently by testosterone when we compare endurance sports with short and explosive sports. In endurance sports, testosterone increases muscle mass, strength and speed so it will be very beneficial for transwomen who participate in these activities.

Lastly, it is important to take into consideration that many studies do not include transwomen because they are challenging to recruit and retain in research studies. Transwomen are more likely to avoid medical care and be excluded from clinical trials that may improve their health, such as screenings for cancer. This may be due to the high cost of hormone therapy or other factors. This can result in a lack of research on hormone therapy's effect on athletic performance of transwomen compared with biological women. There is also a lack of research on how testosterone interacts with estrogen in the muscular system, which is why there are so many unknown factors when discussing the effects of hormones on athletic performance for transwomen.

Ethical and moral concerns raised regarding the use of HRT for cisgender women with athletic aspirations. Some say that testosterone promotes unhealthy eating habits, which is often associated with obesity. This can lead to other problems like osteoporosis and cardiovascular problems. The American Academy of Family Physicians (AAFP) advises caution in the use of HRT for women interested in athletics.

A 2010 study reviewed the ethical issues surrounding HRT amongst transgender individuals: "While transgender-specific hormone therapy can be a significant improvement for many individuals, there are also potential adverse effects that need to be considered when deciding to prescribe hormone therapy for transgender individuals.

CHAPTER 4: MALE ADVANTAGES

Transwomen experience male privileges before transitioning and after transitioning.

Male privilege is when males can experience life without thinking about gender norms or stereotypes. Within the world of sports, there are different types of male advantages due to testosterone levels. These differences are not just physical but also psychological, behavioral and cognitive as well as social and cultural. The biological basis for male advantage in sports which stems from testosterone can be seen in studies such as Malarkey et al., 1989 who studied female athletes who had undergone ovarian transplantation from male donors, showing female athletes had better performance after ovarian transplantation from male donors compared to those that came from females or no donor at all.

This study also shows how physiological advantages can be achieved through male testosterone that is transferred to the female via the ovarian transplantation.

Transwomen who have higher levels of testosterone than biological women will have a greater competitive advantage in certain sports such as running, power lifting and weightlifting because these are sports which require greater muscle mass and bone density. Physical fitness is also greatly affected by hormones, especially androgens; this is evident in the difference in athletic performance between transwomen and biological women even when they have similar testosterone levels.

Additionally, transwomen usually have an advantage over biological women as their body composition changes with hormone replacement therapy, resulting in less fat accumulation and more lean body mass due to their higher level of testosterone.

Men's opinions carry more weight in society than women's do, even when women have more expertise on the topic in question

This is especially true in sports. The idea that men are stronger, faster and better athletes than women is deeply entrenched. There is no scientific basis for this opinion, but it has been perpetuated since 1896 when psychologist C.S. Hagen wrote: "It may be taken as axiomatic that a woman cannot excel in strength ... while the highest degree of muscular development [in a woman] is not much less than 20 percent less than the average man." This idea has been widely accepted as fact, without any proof. The AAFP recommends that this opinion be revised due to the lack of evidence.

Men have been historically placed in positions of dominant authority, power and control in the world of sports. Sports were once considered masculine dominated activities with women playing supportive roles but today, they are more equally shared along gender lines

However, many sports are still dominated by men including Intercollegiate sports, professional sports such as football, baseball and basketball and corporate sponsored sports such as golf and tennis.

There are also many social trends that have contributed to men's dominance in these areas. Socioeconomic trends such as the male breadwinner model have resulted in men having more opportunities for learning new skills and earning higher wages than women thus contributing to their dominance. In addition to this, women are rarely encouraged or chosen to play sports in scholastic or professional sports due to their gender.

Social views of gender differences also contribute to the differences seen in men's and women's sports. People believe that men are naturally stronger and more athletic than women since they have higher muscle mass, strength and flexibility.

In order for these ideals to be challenged and changed, it is necessary for people to become aware of the biological basis for male advantages within sports as well as social factors that perpetuate male dominance over women within sports today.

In addition, there is no consensus on what constitutes "high" testosterone levels in women. Some researchers do not see a difference between transwomen and biological women when it comes to athletic performance. Additionally, some researchers believe that classifying testosterone levels in transwomen as high merely because they are higher than biological women are not appropriate either since there are different genetic backgrounds that may affect how each woman will react to the same dose of hormones.

Transgender athletes share a similar experience to transgender people in general:

Transgender individuals have traditionally been excluded from professional sports due to gender stereotypes. These stereotypes are often reinforced by social views and the media. There are fewer than 100 openly transgender athletes who have participated in international competitions. Some of the reasons for this include;

Transgender women are often considered inferior to cisgender women, especially when it comes to sports.

Social attitudes towards transgender people may also affect their participation in competitive athletics. Some people believe that transwomen are men who have simply left their female bodies behind and do not receive the same attention and recognition as "real" men. Even though transwomen do not necessarily have male anatomy, they can still be perceived as such due to societal views that gender identity is immutable. This results in transwomen being viewed with disdain by other athletes, especially if they are competing against biological women.

When a man gets angry, he is typically seen as powerful and controlling while people see female anger as irrational or hysterical

In a male dominated society, people believe that men are better suited to be leaders. This attitude is evident in sports as well. For example, the women's World Cup has been called the "world's biggest gigglefest" by men who are not supportive of the women's team.

This biased attitude towards sports leads to more negative attitudes towards transwomen participating in certain sports as they receive less respect and do not have equal opportunity as their cisgender counterparts because they are perceived as being less worthy.

Transgender athletes face several challenges when participating in sports such as a lack of acceptance from other athletes and medical professionals. Many people still have misconceptions about transgender people which leads to discrimination and violence against them. Transgender individuals are often excluded from sports leagues or denied access to playing in both male and female leagues. In professional sports, transgender females who compete against biological women face even greater discrimination. For instance, a high school team in Redding, California was barred from participating in their high school's athletic league because of a rule banning transgender athletes from competing on teams with which the athlete identifies with. This is a very common occurrence among transwomen that have attempted to play on teams with other transwomen but almost never occurs in the case of biological women that crossdress or perform first class masquerades.

Transgender individuals are often not taken seriously when they try to participate in sports due to the misconception that their body does not match their true gender identity. This misconception is often reinforced by others as well. Many transwomen have been banned from sports due to their sex assigned at birth which was listed on their identification card rather than by their current identity.

Athletes who are born male but identified as females prior to transitioning face similar challenges in other sports because they are required to compete against biological women, which gives them a competitive disadvantage.

Not all transgender athletes take hormones or get surgery but some choose to do so. This can lead many people who judge transgender individuals based on how they look.

IN PUBLIC SPACES MEN FEEL ENTITLED TO THEIR BODY SPACE WHEREAS WOMEN OFTEN FEEL VIOLATED WHEN MEN TAKE OVER THEIR BODY SPACE

While a woman may be getting harassed by a man, she can usually just try to ignore the offender and keep walking. She has the ability to just walk away and avoid the situation, but when this occurs to a transwoman it's much more difficult for them because people will often use force in order to make her move out of their body space.

A transgender female is not always seen as being female due to stereotypes within society which associate specific physical traits with masculinity and femininity such as breast development, muscle mass and skin tone.

The transgender community is highly affected by social attitudes. Many people believe that transgender women are "not really women" due to their changing physical appearance. This often leads to violence and discrimination against the transgender community and can have a negative effect on their mental health. In a study of 1200 transwomen, 73% of them had attempted suicide at least once due to discrimination from society such as pressure from parents, peers and workmates or being assaulted because of their gender identity.

Transgender athletes face many challenges when participating in sports where they are required to compete against their biological sex.

Men are less likely to become the victim of violent crimes whereas women are more likely to be victims

Transgender females are often victims of sexual assault and domestic violence. In 2011, a study found that 41% of transwomen experienced at least one incident of physical and/or sexual assault in their lifetime.

A 2005 study showed that transwomen were more likely to experience an increased risk of domestic violence when they live with children but do not have legal access to their own name and gender marker on their birth certificate like a married heterosexual couple would.

When a person's name and gender marker are not recognized by authorities or law enforcement, it raises the risk that they will be discriminated against by these institutions.

Many transgender individuals do not receive medical treatment for their gender dysphoria. In a study of 1000 transwomen, only 13% were on HRT. In addition, transgender individuals who are denied medical treatment are more likely to attempt suicide. Many researchers believe that the lack of treatment can lead to depression and other mental health problems which makes it difficult to transition successfully.

People who are denied medical treatment will have a harder time transitioning successfully for many reasons including their lower quality of life and higher risk in committing suicide. One study found that people who were denied medical treatment had more negative feelings towards their bodies than those who received medical treatment and were able to transition successfully without any problems.

One reason that transgender women often do not receive medical treatment is because of their inability to pass as a biological woman due to their different physical appearance. Different research has found that on average, it takes a transgender female much longer to pass as a biological woman than a cisgender man would take to pass as a female.

For example, in one study, an individual who was trying to transition successfully took five years on average from the time they began HRT until they were able to pass completely as biologically female with minimal medications.

The same study found that it would take a cisgender male less than six months to pass as female on average.

One reason that transgender individuals may not receive medical treatment is because it can be difficult to access it. Many doctors do not understand transgenderism or are prejudiced against their patients who have this condition. Additionally, many doctors are not properly trained to assess the need for medical treatment of gender dysphoria, which means that they may deny them if they do not meet all of the requirements in order for treatment to be given.

CHAPTER 5: ADVANTAGES IN THE SOCIETY

This accords them the same privileges that are accorded to men in the society. This also comes under the definition of male privilege.

When a transgender individual passes as male, they are often seen as being more powerful and dominant because of the role that society has assigned to males in society. This is because people tend to associate with those who are seen as the strongest and most dominant people in a society. According to Crenshaw, "… although no one is born with a gender, one's gender identity becomes 'assigned' at birth based on physical characteristics (such as sex-stereotyped genitals) or on behaviors that suggest stereotypical gender roles (such as wearing dresses or playing with dolls)." In the social constructionist approach, an individual's gender is viewed as having been assigned by society at birth. This is in contrast to the essentialist approach, which holds that individuals have innate gender identities. For example, many people hold the belief that an individual's sex is determined by their external genitalia. According to this approach, an individual born with what is commonly referred to as male genitalia must be a boy or a man and vice versa for those born with female genitalia.

Under this view, a baby born with male genitalia and is identified as a boy should be raised as such and receive the same privileges that are accorded to boys in society.

For example, girls who play basketball may be seen as tomboys while boys who play soccer are considered normal for their gender role within society. Girls who wear skirts and makeup are considered butch while boys who do the same are considered gay. Many people believe that traditional gender roles in society must be protected and upheld for the benefit of society as a whole. Therefore, it is viewed as being illegitimate for an adult to cross-dress or to have a gender identity that does not correspond with their biological sex which may contradict stereotypical gender roles that are prevalent throughout the culture.

Gender roles shape one's expectations of themselves (i.e., "shoulds"), their abilities (i.e., "can'ts"), and other people's expectations of them (i.e., "musts"). When one is raised in a society that promotes certain gender roles, gender roles shape one's expectations. For example, a girl who does not fit most of the stereotypes associated with being a girl may grow up to have deep-seated anxieties about her physical appearance because she will have been forced to conform to these "musts" for female gender roles and expectations. As mentioned earlier, gender roles are standardized by society, and may be reinforced through the media.

One of the advantages of having male privilege is that transwomen are viewed as "real men". This is because of the stereotype that manliness is valued over femininity which accords them more privilege and power in society.

Another benefit is that transwomen are discriminated against less than a minority of the transgender population. The cisgender individual is often viewed as being more valued than the transgender individual. This is because they are able to pass and have access to many different privileges in society.

Transwomen also receive equal treatment from other sporting organizations whether it be male or female sports leagues. A study done by the University of California at San Francisco about discrimination in sports found that transwomen were welcomed into women's leagues just like cisgender females when there was an issue with athletes being too masculine or femininity being too soft for their desired gender identity and/or expression during competition.

Transwomen are able to use the same locker rooms and bathrooms as females within the sports arena. This is because of the lack of discrimination that transwomen receive when they are able to pass as male.

Transgender athletes who are born male but identify as female prior to transitioning face many challenges when participating in the same sports that cisgender females compete in. They are required to compete against biological females, which gives them a competitive disadvantage. This inequality is common among all transgender athletes, but transwomen often do not receive equal treatment in sports leagues due to their lower status and less negative perception of them than cisgender males.

Many people believe that transgender individuals are not real women and that they should not be allowed to compete against biological females. This is due to misconceptions about transgenderism based on misinformation. Some of the most common misconceptions about transgenderism include:

Many people who are intolerant of transwomen do not believe that they deserve their place in society because their gender identity does not match their physiological sex and the way society defines what a female should look like. People who express these strong sentiments often intend to harm transwomen because of their gender identity, but also feel threatened by them because of how different they look compared to cisgender females.

CHAPTER 6: MENTAL ADVANTAGES

Transwomen are likely to have an easier time identifying and dealing with their emotions

Apart from the physical advantages that transwomen may have on biological women, there also exist psychological differences between them. This is what leads to the claim that transgender women are biologically better put together than cis women. These psychological differences include: gender role socialization (the way that males and females conform their behavior to perceived gender roles), hormonal profile (levels of testosterone and estrogen) and endocrine system development (hormones such as estrogen can masculinize the brain). Gender role socialization has been shown to play a major role in how an individual's body develops. Transwomen are often more psychologically durable than their cisgender counterparts due to the way that they are treated by society. They are often perceived as "real men" by society and therefore encouraged to develop masculine traits in their personality. This leads to many transwomen being able to deal well with the higher levels of social stigma they face compared to transwomen who do not conform with society's stereotyped gender roles.

Hormone levels are also an important factor when it comes to psychological health among transgender women. The hormone most associated with masculinity is testosterone, which is considered to be one reason for the increased aggressiveness reported by cisgender men. On the contrary, the hormone estrogen has been reported to have a positive effect on mood in women. Transwomen have higher levels of estrogen in their bodies and lower levels of testosterone because they are able to access treatment for their condition. This may be why many researchers believe that transwomen would perform better psychologically than cisgender women because they deal better with stress and anxiety when they are able to pass as male without receiving any medical treatment.

The formation of an endocrine system begins at conception when an individual is exposed to hormones and can be affected before birth. Transwomen are able to access HRT therapy before their birth because they are in fact the same person that they were years ago. They are able to do this without any major surgery or medical treatment, which may be why many researchers believe that transwomen would perform better psychologically than cisgender women because they deal better with stress and anxiety when they are able to pass as male without receiving any medical treatment.

Many transwomen can become pregnant and raise children successfully. This has been shown to be possible through adoption, fertility reversal, sperm donation or egg donation; however, one of the best methods is by undergoing hysterectomy and oophorectomy in order to make their own body conform more closely to their gender expression.

In a study done by the University of California at San Francisco, thirty-nine percent of transgender women who were seeking treatment had experienced some form of abuse that might have impacted their psychological well-being. This was considered much higher than the rate for cisgender women who experienced abuse (an average of 14 percent). It was even higher than the rate for other transgender individuals (an average of 17 percent).

The results suggested that transwomen's abuse history could be a contributing factor to their psychological well-being and that social support may be helpful.

In another study done by the same university, transgender women who had experienced violence were 3.5 times more likely than their non-abused transgender female counterparts to have attempted suicide (the rate being 9 percent for the non-abused group and 37 percent for the abused group). Transgender women are also more likely than cisgender men to have attempted suicide (an average of 4 percent versus 1–2 percent). Transwomen are also more likely than cisgender women to have attempted suicide (an average of 7.8 percent versus 2.6%).

Transwomen who have not undergone surgery are more likely to attempt suicide, but results show that those who have undergone treatment for their condition are more likely to improve their quality of life. This is especially true if the person in question has had any form of social support.

CHAPTER 7: THEORETICAL AND PHILOSOPHICAL ASPECTS

Transgenderism has been referred to as a disorder because it does not conform with the biological determinism present in society. This means that an individual's gender identity does not match up with their biological sex and therefore claims that individuals who have this condition have a mental illness. This proclamation has been criticized by many researchers because it does not take into consideration that an individual's gender identity is in fact, a part of the human experience.

Gender identity formation involves the recognition of one's own gender. The term "gender" is sometimes used as shorthand to refer to the attitudes, feelings and behaviors that a given culture associates with a given sex. In other words, gender is a set of psychological and behavioral tendencies that are commonly attributed to women and men. A trans person may experience their own gender identity as different from their birth sex. This phenomenon is referred to as gender dysphoria.

Gender identity can be described as how a person subjectively feels and experiences their own gender. It is influenced by biological factors, as well as psychological, social and cultural factors. There are several transwomen who do not feel that they are women, but rather feel that they are male or neither male nor female. This is known as non-binary transgenderism and currently the theory behind this is the lack of a "real" woman in society.

The idea that gender identity is a "set of psychological and behavioral tendencies" has been criticized by some researchers, including Janice Raymond, who in her book "The Transsexual Empire" (1990) argues that the study of transsexuality is an attempt to construct and maintain a gender system which may be robbing people of their own naturally felt gender/sexual identities.

A very common criticism of transwomen is that they are really only pretending to be women. This criticism stems from the belief that their body does not match up with what society defines as female. For example, because some transwomen have masculine features, they are viewed as fake women who are fooling other females by claiming to be female when they are actually male.

Another criticism of transwomen is that they are male and therefore cannot really know what it is like to be a woman. Many people feel that because transwomen have a penis, they cannot have the proper qualifications to understand what it is like to be a woman. This criticism stems from the belief that being female requires certain physical features, such as having breasts.

Many people who are intolerant of transwomen do not believe that they deserve their place in society because their gender identity does not match up with their physiological sex and the way society defines what a female should look like. They often intend to harm transwomen because of their gender identity, but also feel threatened by them because of how different they look compared to cisgender females.

CLOSING THOUGHTS

As seen throughout this book, it is without a doubt true that transwomen have an advantage over cis women when it comes to some sports. It is also true that transwomen on Hormone Replacement therapy have significantly reduced levels of testosterone, and increased levels of estrogen. In addition to this, they also have reduced levels of hair growth and decreased bone density. The question that is raised from this is whether or not transwomen should be allowed to compete in sporting events as if they were cisgender women. Some people believe that they should not be allowed to compete because their body does not conform with what society defines as the ideal female body type. Other people believe that transwomen should be allowed to compete because their physique has been altered due to hormone replacement therapy, which has made them more similar to cisgender women than before HRT treatment.

'For the Olympic level, the elite level, I'd say probably two years is more realistic than one year," said the study's lead author, Dr. Timothy Roberts, a pediatrician and the director of the adolescent medicine training program at Children's Mercy Hospital in Kansas City, Missouri. "At one year, the transwomen on average still have an advantage over the cis women," he said. "So if we're going purely by height and weight, then yes, we're going to have some very big transwomen and some very small cis women. But that's not a level playing field."

Transwomen may be at an advantage from the testosterone they were born with, but after HRT treatment, their testosterone levels drop to close to female normal ranges for their age group.

Some scientists believe that this is enough time to allow the athlete to compete in sports against cisgender females because their testosterone levels are no longer higher than what is expected for female athletes.

How is it fair for a person who has been on HRT treatment to compete against other female athletes? Scientists have recently published an article claiming that reducing testosterone to female normal levels in transwomen allows them to compete fairly against cisgender females. This study claims that transwomen who have undergone HRT treatment are so close in size and performance metrics to their cisgender counterparts that they should be allowed to compete as if they were cisgender females.

If competitive advantage is the only factor to be used to determine whether transwomen should be allowed in female events, we must consider also that there are other differences between women. For example, left-handed basketballers have been shown to have an advantage over their right-handed colleagues yet this is not a factor that is used to discriminate against them. It is also possible that some cisgender females can have testosterone levels higher than those who are allowed to compete and still be allowed to play basketball. In addition, to the advantage of height, some cisgender women are naturally taller than others.

www.ingramcontent.com/pod-product-compliance
Lightning Source LLC
Chambersburg PA
CBHW060919130726
48001CB00006B/2320